AF415942

Learning techniques & learning methods in studies

How to learn faster, remember better and write top grades in a relaxed manner with effective learning strategies and perfect time management.

Lukas Glaser

CONTENT

What you can expect in this book

Are you about to start studying and are you already feeling a good dose of creeping overwhelm in addition to anticipation at the thought of it? Have you just started and need some guidance on how to balance your studies and your free time as well as possible? Have you been wishing for a fresh start for a long time because the recurring cycle of motivation, procrastination and stressful learning is draining you? Do you no longer know what your real problem is and how to tackle it? Don't despair yet, because the knowledge you'll gain in this book can turn your entire studies upside down.

This book takes a step-by-step approach to the problems that stand between you and greater success in your studies. Starting with your basic perspective, motivation, and procrastination, you will learn to build a routine that is tailored to you and will protect you from sudden bulimic learning. Explanations of your internal and external structure will help you filter out and address your difficulties in organization and time management. Tips on how to increase your attention in classes or work more efficiently on your own at home will allow you to have a balanced daily life by not missing out on your hobbies. Strategies for simplifying learning and reproducing content and working efficiently through texts provide you with concrete, applicable solutions.

Finally, you'll find a ten-point plan in this book that you can start working on right away, and a list of recommended reading if you want to explore certain topics in more depth. In the end, you'll learn that you don't necessarily have to work harder, but for the most part, just smarter.

Common problems in everyday study

In the everyday life of a student, there can be various problems, but the same problem areas always arise: lack of motivation, lack of organization, chaotic preparation for exams and difficulties in mastering the course material. In the following, we will therefore look at motivation and procrastination, structure formation and time management, and various working and learning strategies.

TOO LITTLE MOTIVATION AND TOO MUCH PROCRASTINATION

Motivation

In the beginning was motivation. Or perhaps: In the beginning was the desire for motivation? The course of study has been chosen, you've moved into your shared apartment, and perhaps you already have a rough idea of what might come after graduation. Full of drive, you set to work in the first semester - and there is so much to discover! The university campus, the course formats, lecturers, fellow students and all in all a new life.

But little by little, small signs of wear and tear begin to show. Whether during the cramming for the first exams or in later semesters - it becomes increasingly clear that this new life also brings with it a large chunk of personal responsibility. Whereas in school there was a fixed timetable, clear homework was assigned and there was usually enough time to meet friends or do other leisure activities, now the follow-up work doesn't do itself, the flatmates demand their attention and you've wanted to do sports for a while. Who has time for additional texts, follow-up work or office hours?

For a few more weeks and months you try to juggle everything, and again and again some balls fall to the ground, until you finally ask yourself why you are struggling at all. Gone are the anticipation, the thirst for knowledge, and the inspiring career idea. In their place is now a daily routine in which working through things and hoping that nothing and no one comes up short is the main focus. So how can the motivation from the beginning be found again?

Find motivation

As with many other things, the first step out of a deadlock - whatever that may be - is the first step. Something has to change. But what? That's exactly what you need to become aware of. How do you feel when you think about your studies? What thought comes to your mind about free time? No matter where you want to start, try to listen to yourself openly and honestly and pay attention to the first impulses that come to you. Of course, you can do this by talking to someone close to you. You can also record your thoughts and feelings in writing - whether organized or unorganized. Mindmaps are also a good idea if you can think of several problem areas at once.

Now it is a matter of acting as quickly as possible.

Up to this point, you had become accustomed to a routine and it is only human that breaking with it meets with inner reluctance. This is not necessarily because you are not convinced that something should change, but merely because the human brain likes habits. Consequently, something new always involves a certain amount of effort. Sometimes we hardly notice it. We see a nice dance movie, are impressed, and sign up for a class the very next day.

Why is it so easy? Because here the activation energy came through inspiration. This is exactly the energy that should be preserved and used by responding as quickly as possible to one of your impulses. If you don't, it becomes more and more likely that the thought of change will slip further and further into the subconscious and become the things you should maybe do at some point when you have nothing else to do at the moment. So never.

Therefore: Listen to yourself, become aware of what you want to do, and act on it as quickly as possible. Keep it as concrete as possible. For example, if you find that you can't keep up in a seminar because the instructor keeps building on concepts from secondary literature that you don't know, make a resolution to read at least one text from it before each seminar and write it down in your planner immediately. If there is no official reading list, make a note to ask for it before the next session - or better yet, compose a brief email to the instructor immediately. Once you have a concrete goal and muster the necessary activation energy, the stone will quickly roll by itself.

The information and support to achieve your goal can soon be found as if by itself via books in the university library, explanatory and advice videos on the Internet, or fellow members of your social circle. The key to motivation is responding to stimuli.

Get motivation?

But motivation is not enough in the long run. Although the phrase "I just can't motivate myself to study regularly" is a much-heard one, it actually describes a problem that doesn't have much to do with motivation. The impulse and the goal are there, and probably some steps have been taken to look at notes more often and not just start reviewing a few days before exams, but where it falters is incorporating it all into everyday life. There is no routine.

Motivation is good for giving direction, but it only helps for a short time. As already described, the brain prefers to take the easier path than the difficult one when faced with a decision. The law of least effort and resistance applies. This means that this tendency to make things easier must be actively overcome again and again when relying on motivation alone. Mental energy and willpower must be gathered again and again in order not to deviate from the original intention. This, however, consumes an enormous amount of energy over time and so one soon notices how one falls back into old habits. The notes are packed away after the course and not taken out again until the next session.

This is comparable to the annual observable phenomenon of gyms. At New Year's, many people resolve to live healthier and exercise more. They are highly motivated to achieve their dream figure by summer, sign up at the gym and take as many classes as possible. But by the end of spring, the contract cancellations are already coming in. Changing everything all at once is harder than you thought and can't be done with a mental snap of the fingers alone.

So how can the initial motivation be used and how can a change succeed in everyday life? By following up on the decision to change something with the way to get there also being integrated into everyday life and established as the standard. In other words, new habits must be created. This is the only way to relieve the brain of the decision to do something initially unpleasant, so that this can happen automatically.

Consequently, what is the path from motivation to habits to achieving personal goals? Here is a step-by-step flow chart:

1. Observe your daily routine and build in your change realistically. For example, if you want to study more for a specific course, consider which days of the week you really have time for it. In this way, you enable your plan to actually become a habit, and you don't run the risk that it will have to avoid other important things that also have their place in your everyday life.

2. Start small. Hardly anything can set you back more than being overwhelmed. So take smaller steps at first. You have time one afternoon a week to review the material? Great! Make a resolution to study for half an hour on this day every week. This way, you can start working on your goal right away without it being too much for you to handle right from the start. Still, you have the metaphorical foot in the door. This allows you to slowly get used to the change. Over time, you can then build up to it gradually. When you realize that it's simple for you to sit down to study for the half hour

each week, take it a step further. Build your new habit gradually and move to looking at your notes for three quarters of an hour now, for example.

3. Make the change as effortless as possible for yourself. Connected to the sequential approach is that you should try to take tension concerning the upcoming change out of the situation. This works best by adapting and preparing what pertains to the new habit. That half hour of studying scheduled? Make sure your notes are neat and organized. Have an uncluttered workspace that is customized to your needs. Remove distractions like notifications from your phone, distracting noises, or open tabs to videos you'd rather be watching than doing your work.

4. Expect difficulties. It is only normal to encounter problems or even failure when dedicating yourself to something new. It's no different when developing habits. Accept that mistakes and fallibilities may come your way, and don't let them upset you if they do occur. Don't give up if, after a few weeks, you still haven't gotten around to studying in the afternoon. Remember that progress is a process, so it has to build up. Take a breath, think about what the mistake was, how it came about, and learn from it. Perhaps draw the consequence of spending at least another ten minutes on

your notes that day in the evening. If you come out of such situations without immediately throwing everything away, this will strengthen you in the long run.

Procrastination

So-called procrastination describes the process in which it is very clear what is supposed to be done, but other tasks or activities are pushed forward instead.

These are accompanied by flimsy excuses and explanations. I can't start learning like this just yet. Everything here is still full of unwashed clothes. If it's tidier, I'm sure it will be easier for me. Besides, I have the whole afternoon to get started. The half hour will also find itself later". Unfortunately, as we all know, in the end it doesn't turn up, or only forced to, with considerable effort that should actually be avoided, and feelings of guilt because you could have started earlier.

Procrastination is well known and probably everyone has experienced it. But contrary to the common assumption that procrastination is due to laziness and unwillingness, this phenomenon is actually an avoidance maneuver. We usually procrastinate when we are simply overwhelmed by the task in front of us, and there are a number of things we can do about it.

First, work on **becoming aware** that and when you procrastinate. Listen to yourself and realize that your excuses, while logical, do not justify why deviate from the original plan.

Observe which tasks you start procrastinating on and think about what the reason is. Being overwhelmed can have different reasons, but it's basically because the task you wanted to tackle is too big. Studying for a full half hour this afternoon doesn't seem feasible. **Consequently, concretize and downsize your goals** for next time. Instead, say to yourself, "I'm going to go back over my notes from the last session of the seminar for fifteen minutes this afternoon at 3:00."

Then try to **let go of** any **feelings of guilt that** arise. Accept your small temporary failure, forgive yourself, and move on. You are no less created for your tasks just because they once felt too big for you and your brain reacted in a simply human way by avoiding them. **Create Momentum**. Fine, maybe you would have wanted to start reviewing material an hour ago, but there's nothing stopping you from getting to it right now and doing at least a little bit.

Once you start, it will be much easier for you to stick with it and possibly finish the task before you. The same helps with blockages caused by too much brooding. Try not to think too much beforehand about whether you have all the tools you need to master the task, and don't get carried away with self-doubt and questions about how best to get started. Something is better than nothing in this case and can always be revised afterwards.

Similarly, if you know you're putting something off because it's hard for you. Intentionally start **working on the hard thing first**. Sit down to the task and do at least something on it, thus making it easier for you to start again later and stop when you need a break. You still have the most energy at the beginning of your work phase. Besides, you know that after that it can only get easier with other tasks.

Last but not least, a prepared **energy pack** can also help you break out of a procrastination rut. Gather a few things that inspire you and remind you why you need to face more unpleasant problem sometimes on your way. This can be a board with beautiful photos on the topic, handy symbols that stand for your goal, motivating texts or inspiring movies. There are no limits for you!

TOO MUCH CHAOS

Now you have learned what you need to get to work. You are ready to start, but you should also think about your external requirements for a successful study. That's why this chapter will be about organizing a suitable workspace and structuring your habits.

Workplace tidiness

You've already encountered procrastination as a symptom of being overwhelmed. Accordingly, it is not surprising that a cluttered environment can also make us work less efficiently or perhaps not get to work properly in the first place. Thus, a workspace that is orderly for you is essential. That doesn't mean it has to be minimalistically set up, clinically clean, or always in the same place at all. Try the following suggestions and adapt them to your personal needs.

Your workplace should be **organized** and kept as **clean** as possible. Nothing is suddenly easier to deal with than pieces of paper or cake crumbs lying around, even though that one important chapter should actually be read through. Cables to the laptop or computer should not tangle on the table and also leave enough space for the materials you will be working with. It is also beneficial to think about the exact placement of your technical devices so that, if necessary, you can use them at the same time as a notebook without encountering spatial problems.

The place should create a **pleasant atmosphere for** you so that you don't want to work on your tasks simply because you feel uncomfortable. Get creative.

Do you get cold feet quickly and that's why you want to put a soft carpet underneath? Do you like certain smells and therefore think about a scented candle? There are no limits for you. It is also beneficial to have something of your personal energy package as **inspiration** in the visual field. This can be done, for example, via a photo wall.

Furthermore, you should have everything you need within **easy reach** so that you have to interrupt your workflow as little as possible. Consequently, this includes not only your planner, books, notes, and writing utensils, but you should also think of something to drink, possibly a small snack, or tissues, for example, if it's spring right now and you suffer from hay fever. It also includes some kind of **overview of the** things you want to tackle - be it a planner, a big calendar or a to-do list.

The last big thing you should do is **remove distractions.** Escape interruptions from notifications and group chats and put your phone away. Go into airplane mode - as often as you can - with your tech devices. Also, make sure you have good light, either by sitting next to a window or by setting up a desk lamp - even in addition.

Finally, sounds around you can also be distracting. Experiment with white noise or even noise interference, instrumental or ambient music to help you concentrate and focus. If you always choose the same accompaniment, this can have the added benefit of making the music work for you as a trigger to the work phase. Only music that is particularly text-heavy or that encourages you to move should be left alone and saved for your breaks. Try yourself out!

Sitting for long periods is not good for people or for your concentration. Therefore, make sure that you set up your workplace as **ergonomically** as possible. To do this, first adjust your chair. When sitting upright, your forearms should rest straight on the tabletop without too much weight on them. You should place your mouse and keyboard where your hands will automatically land. If your knees are now bent at an angle of more than 90 degrees, then help out with a footstool, a stack of paper or books so that you can sit stably.

After that, it's all about your monitor. This should be an arm's length away from your body so that you can read what's on the screen without straining. Also, the top edge of the screen should be level with your eyes. Again, different objects can be used to accomplish this. There are special laptop raisers, under which the absolutely advised external mouse and keyboard can be conveniently stored, in case the device is not used, but should remain in its place.

If you are working on two monitors and one of them is the main monitor, place it directly in front of you. If both are used equally, they should be connected directly in front of you and placed at a slight angle. Last but not least, there should also be some **order** in **your digital workspace.**

Make sure to keep your desktop as empty as possible. Create a logical folder structure for yourself and stick to it. This includes naming files accurately. Put all programs, folders and files that you don't necessarily need on your home screen under this structure. Furthermore, try to clean up your downloads folder once a week, empty the recycle bin and go through the inbox of your email. Also, unsubscribe from any newsletters and advertisements that you no longer need.

It is also advisable to regularly back up your hard

drive - either to a cloud or to an external hard drive. Here, too, once a week is a good rhythm. Finally, it remains to go through your browser bookmarks about once a month and sort out unnecessary ones here as well.

Tidy head

A tidy workplace is probably one of the first things to give structure.

However, it is almost more important that you know exactly where you want to go and how you want to get there. That is why the following section now deals with the systematic preparation of your tasks. In doing so, it is important to keep in mind what was stated in the previous section: Plans and procedures should not only work sometimes or even for a few days. What you are looking for is a process that suits you and creates habits. Accordingly, try out the following tips and analyze what works for you and where you might want to change something.

So overall, consistency and regularity will help you. Both can be achieved primarily by keeping **track of** what needs to be done. Planners, notebooks, calendars or sticky notes can provide this. Work and study plans, mind maps or lists provide a good way of keeping track. Also, try to schedule **repetitions** appropriately in your daily routine. These will make it easier for you to face your tasks. How these can turn out will now be explained.

The realistic work plan

In the search for habits and routines that do not need to be thought about and decided, the way hardly leads around a work plan. The first thing to do is to create an overview of the week.

First of all, all fixed appointments are noted down in it: Courses, leisure activities or cleaning duties in the shared flat. Special events such as doctor's appointments or the birthday party of your best friend should also be included - in principle, everything that is non-negotiable. Unfortunately, if this means that the weekly schedule is already completely exhausted, something has to give way to appointments. If this is the case for every week, it makes sense to consider taking fewer modules.

Once these blocks are in place, rest periods should be considered. This means both small breaks during the day and - if possible - one or two days a week on which no time at all is spent with the university and learning material. Last but not least, phases for self-study and buffer times are built in, in case something should take longer or more time is needed when it comes to exams. These buffer times can also become free time if everything is already done.

When dividing up the work blocks, it is necessary to be aware of when in the day personal productivity phases lie and how long they can last. No one is helped if you start reading texts in an exemplary manner at seven in the morning, if you are then so tired and knackered before noon that you can't manage anything else for the rest of the day.

It is the same with the length of work. Consequently, it makes sense to set yourself work start and end times and thus treat your studies like a job. Observe yourself and realistically assess how your energy balance works - and if you notice after a few weeks that the new rhythm doesn't quite suit you after all, you can always change or adjust it. Take a step-by-step approach.

Now that you have determined when your independent study blocks are, it is time to plan the content of these independent work periods.

A large block should be divided into several small units of about half an hour with breaks in between. This promotes the ability to concentrate in the long run. In addition, the units should alternate as much as possible in terms of their content and the way they are worked on so that boredom does not arise. Therefore, proceed in such a way that you use the so-called SMART way of thinking[1] . When planning the units, ask yourself the following questions so that you know exactly what you want to work on:

• What exactly do I want to get done? Where will I work on it? How will I get started? What materials will I need?

• How will I know when I am finished, e.g. because I have understood everything? Are there possibilities like exercises, tests, quizzes by a fellow student or? Can I explain what I have learned to someone?

• Am I really ready to work in the time I have set aside, or is something else more important at the time? Will I push away my unwillingness to do something?

• How much time do I realistically need to complete my tasks? Will the time allotted be enough? Does it make sense for me to work at this time of day?

• How is the block divided up in terms of time? When does it start? When does it end? When will there be

---

Cf. Charles Duhigg: Smarter, Faster, Better. Why some people get so much done - and others don't. Munich: Redline Verlag 2017, p. 128 ff.

breaks?

The perfect to-do list

Interwoven with the structure of a work plan and the concrete planning of individual units is, of course, the question of what is to be done at all. It doesn't help to have a pile of notes on which tasks have been written down in key words at some point, but now it's no longer clear what was meant for about half of them. It's better to **write down** a big **list of** everything that needs to be done - whether it's an exercise that needs to be thought through again, looking up a term that the lecturer never explains, calling the BAföG office or watching a series that has been recommended for the hundredth time: Everything may be noted down. Even the form can range from bullet points to mind maps, have different color markings and underlining or not. If it has not already been done during the first writing, all major goals should be divided into **small tasks** so that it becomes visible which steps are actually hidden behind the points.

This overall list and its task items can then be used to **flesh out** the respective **weekly plan**. To do this, it's helpful to pick three items that have the highest **priority, for** example, and mark them. What absolutely has to be done this week and can't wait until next week? What needs the most energy and should therefore be done first?

Which tasks have a high personal value because, for example, other people also depend on their completion? The focus should then be on these three actions. Now the overall list should be **regularly assessed and updated** - this can also be worked into the weekly schedule as a fixed date. This is a good opportunity to pat yourself on the back for the things you've completed and ask yourself why others always fall by the wayside. Is there that one item that is never a high priority?

Maybe it is not so relevant in the end and can be deleted again? Did you want to write that email to your professor for weeks, but never really knew how to formulate it and therefore didn't dare? For problems like this, it's a good idea to either get help with the implementation - after all, the professor won't know at the end whether the e-mail has been proofread by a friend - or to schedule the whole thing for the next day with the highest priority - or both together.

The stress-free exam preparation

Such an overall list with sub-goals can also be used wonderfully for exam preparation. As soon as the exam date has been announced, the exam preparation should already begin - at least slowly. The date can be noted in the planner and **planned backwards from** there. The learning deadline should be set generously to have enough buffer in case something like a week in which you didn't get out of bed because of a cold comes up.

Then it should be clarified as soon as possible what is actually part of the **material relevant to the exam.** A visit to the lecturer's office hours can also help here. It also makes sense to know how the knowledge will be tested later. Do short questions have to be answered? Are there selection questions? Will an essay be written? Does evidence have to be kept? All of this can and should influence exactly how you prepare for the exam.

To create the exact learning plan, you should make an **overview of all relevant topic blocks.** This includes the rough topics, names of central concepts and sometimes already core facts and formulas you need. If you are lucky, tutorials are offered in which you can make such an overview or it is already part of the course material. If not, you can either build it yourself from your notes or research it on the internet and in books.

Especially for foundation modules, the probability is relatively high that the same topics are covered in different universities and courses, so you can use the overview as a basis for your own and adapt it.

Think about which **sub-steps** are necessary to prepare the relevant topics for the corresponding exam and their type of query. Do you need to revise and organize your notes? Should you review a secondary work? Do you need to take additional notes? How will you review the material? Are there practice exercises? Are there mock exams? Is there an opportunity for joint correction or discussion in a tutorial or among fellow students?

Finally, make a **learning plan** from your topic overview. Set a goal for the week that has top priority for you. Alternate easy and difficult topics as much as possible and determine when you really want to study which topics intensively. Pay attention to your learning plan and check daily what your current status is so that the plan can be adjusted if necessary.

TOO MUCH TO REMEMBER

You're motivated, you've established a routine, and you've set up a workstation. Now what? What exactly can be done to help you be more successful in your studies? In this chapter, you will learn how to be more effective in your course work and in your independent follow-up, so that you will soon have fewer problems in your everyday university life and in preparing for exams.

From the course ...

Let's start with lectures, seminars and exercises: Twelve years of a fixed schedule and frontal teaching, get used to seeing the teaching-learning situation more as a necessary evil before free time in the afternoon.

A few contents can probably be quite interesting, but all in all rather passively waiting until it goes home again to nicer occupations. Maybe you still do a few tasks at home and repeat then comes a day or two before the exam.

It can't go on like this - unfortunately - at university. Think of your studies as what they are: Your main occupation. Your **studies should be treated like your job**, because that's the only way you'll attach enough relevance to them, and thus to yourself. You don't have to overdo it and assume a 40-hour week or demand even more of yourself, but you should realize that sooner rather than later you won't be able to keep up professionally if you leave it at a few hours of verbal banter a week - and you didn't choose your course of study for no reason! So take it seriously and accept the necessary steps involved. Learn to make necessary and sensible decisions and also to sometimes put aside un-willingness or more fun activities.

First of all, you need to **increase** your **attention and activity in the lectures**. A simple trick here is to sit as far in front of and in the visual field of the lec-turer as possible. It sounds too simple to be true, but it will be more noticeable if you turn to something like the last group chat.

Even without prompting, this will allow you to es-cape such distraction opportunities. In addition, in-structors will be able to interact with you better, so that just a few glances at what you are saying will make you more active. By the way, an alternative for online events from home would be to turn on your camera permanently. This creates a better social climate and, on the lecturer side, it is more quickly noticeable from your reactions whether you have not understood something or want to comment on something. It also makes for much smoother conversations.

This goes hand in hand with **getting to know your teachers to a certain extent**. This is not to say that you should run after them everywhere, no. However, it is beneficial to have some relationship after all. If the teacher knows you, you will automatically try harder, because there will be a certain expectation that you want to meet.

You will shed the feeling of having nothing to do with the person in front of you, and the course and your behavior around it will become a matter of personal concern to you. On a professional level, it is also advisable to take a quick look at what your lecturers mainly deal with.

During the lecture, pay attention not only to the above-mentioned information, but also to the points at which your lecturers linger longer, which terms they repeat or which words they particularly emphasize - in short: decode and analyze behavior and what is said. It's also a good idea to come up with a small system of signs that you can use to mark and emphasize particularly important points in your notes. This will soon give you a much better understanding of what is important and how it is important, and you will be able to prepare for the exam in a much more appropriate way. One last tip: Make a note in the margin of your notes of all the specific questions and short exercises that are asked or discussed. This will show you what style of questioning the lecturer uses, so that you can adapt to it. You can also easily create your own mock exam from the questions you have collected, which will help you prepare for the exam.

Socialize **with fellow students**. At first, this sounds contradictory: How am I supposed to concentrate better if I'm sitting in class chatting with my friends? But this is primarily about your life, which takes place outside the seminars and lectures. Of course, studying is more fun when you know you're going to meet your friends, but you can gain further advantages by creating a network of people who also deal with the same or similar content as you on a daily basis. Such a group - or even just a few people - can support each other by meeting together to study or work.

Plus, you'll have people to turn to when you need help. Having a hard time studying for a certain lecture, understanding a certain concept, or even finding a suitable structure for your daily study routine? Talk about it.

Chances are that others have encountered your

problems themselves and you can find solutions together. You don't know what a specific procedure at the university looks like or you need secondary literature on a certain topic as quickly as possible?

Maybe one of your fellow students has already dealt with this! Last but not least, such a network is also a good way to watch out for each other, to control and build up. If you know that your friends are also studying for this one exam, you will develop a much higher sense of responsibility not to stand in the way and follow along as part of the group. By the way, a group like this doesn't necessarily have to meet every day in the dining hall or lecture hall. Also look online for groups in social networks that have a similar daily routine as you and share your interest in your field of study.

Design transcripts

You are sitting in one of the first rows of the lecture, you have your friends, with whom you will talk through the material afterwards, next to you, you are actively listening to the lecturer - but how do you take notes? There are, of course, various methods: from digital to handwritten; from sparse bullet points to symbolic drawings to detailed sentences. Of course, you should also observe and analyze which is the appropriate style for you and the event in question. Nevertheless, there are some points that are always helpful.

Even if it sounds outdated: **write by hand**. The physical process helps you and your brain interact more actively with the information and ultimately remember it. Additionally, handwriting has the advantage that you can rephrase, add to, and be freer with your notes right away.

It is difficult to insert your own short notes, marginal notes or little pictures into a digital document simultaneously with the lecture, so that you will completely negate these interactions with the material, which are helpful for memorization. If you are reluctant to work mainly with pen and paper, at least have a sheet of paper on which you briefly record your thoughts, questions, or relevant terms of the topics covered.

From the beginning, keep your **notes so that they form the basis of your exam preparation**. You should not just record what was said. This means: think about a heading and marking system beforehand. Do you want to number through, sort by color, use different underlining? A small character set can also be very helpful. This way you can mark in a uniform and clear way which notes contain, for example, examples, terminology or central concepts. These points should definitely be highlighted in some way - either directly during the course or when revising your notes.

It is also possible to design the first page of your notes as a **table of contents.** Here you can continuously enter how the topics are arranged among themselves and where they can be found again. Page numbers are helpful, but not absolutely necessary.

Make marginal notes as described earlier. Follow the course carefully, noting, for example, when something is emphasized. There is a high probability that this is a basal term, an essential formula, an important topic, or a relevant concept. You should also note the questions asked by the teaching staff. Also make notes where you did not understand something. You can then ask these follow-up questions much more easily after the session or in office hours than if you have to remember them first or only remember shortly before the exam that there were still uncertainties about a topic.

In the end, you can make excellent use of the preceding highlighting and marginal notes for your exam preparation. Create a **small study outline or notebook**. During the semester, work on a bullet-point overview of the corresponding course. This can also consist of just the structured headings of the sessions. You can also add key terminology or facts. Edit this outline so that it becomes your guide for planning exam preparation.

... for self-study

The session is over. What happens now in the time that you can dispose of yourself?

Create efficient habits

If there's one thing you should take away, it's this: build a good routine. Here are common and daily actions you can do to make your studies more successful. Some of the things might sound familiar from what we covered earlier. Here they are, in part, summarized again.

General activities first include your relationship with the subject of study. Work **steadily** rather than with quick fixes that will only make you expend more energy in the long run.

Stay **organized**. Create an environment that motivates you to learn, for example, by involving fellow students or friends in your goals and ways to achieve them.

This creates a kind of **social accountability**

where you are no longer solely on your own. In these groups, the **learning material** can **also** be **wonderfully analyzed** and thought through. If you develop fun with the content, it will also be much easier for you to remember it. **Actively engage with the new knowledge by** independently researching specific concepts in various media, if necessary. You will be amazed at the graphics and explanatory videos that are freely available on the Internet alone. This will also make the content more accessible to you, easier to understand and effortless to remember. In addition, you should make sure to **keep yourself fit**. Regular exercise helps you stay more alert and active, but even light exercise such as walks increases concentration and memory. The next time your head is spinning, simply step outside for ten minutes and then get back to work refreshed.

In addition, it's a good idea to exercise your brain as well, not just use it for material from classes. Look for gentle stimulation in your free time, whether that's Sudokus, books, or something else. However, breaks are also necessary. At the end of the day, ensure undisturbed, healthy sleep. Fixed periods of rest and dreaming will, on the one hand, make your routine daily life easier and, on the other hand, make you more efficient in the long run.

When it comes specifically to learning and repeating content, it is considerable to let the **new knowledge run** through your mind again in the **first 24 hours** after you have covered it. This can take a variety of forms. For example, you can talk about it with friends, read through your transcripts again, or transfer points you've already made to your learning review. It is entirely up to you. The main thing is to review the learning while the memory of the session is fresh. Try to **learn contextually as** well.

This means that you create certain triggers for attentive knowledge acquisition. Visually, for example, this can mean that you always design your learning environment in a similar way, for example by always arranging your writing materials and other materials in the same way on your seat.

You can also change this structure as you wish depending on the course and then repeat it at home as you study each session.

In addition, you should **repeat the** acquired **knowledge in different places**. This may sound contradictory to the previous point at first, but it revolves around remembering the learning material in different ways in different situations. As a result, your brain will not simply associate the content with sitting in a dull lecture hall, but will internalize that you want to interact with it. Using the knowledge frequently means it will be better stored as relevant to you and will remain retrievable more quickly. Just be sure to give yourself rest periods, too! Work steadily on your **learning overview** and, along with your **exam preparation plan,** review where you are and what still needs to be done - and not just the week before the exam, but stringently throughout the semester.

When it comes to concrete exam preparation, make it as active as possible. **Practice the question situation** by taking as many mock exams as possible. Write your own tests if necessary. Think through covered problems again and check to see if you arrive at the same results. Have fellow students ask you specific questions about the subject matter and see to what extent you can explain concepts freely and coherently. In short, expose yourself to tests and possible errors before the all-important deadline.

Rituals you can do daily are:

• **Scroll through the next two months in your planner**. This way, you always have important deadlines or goals in front of you and make sure you don't miss anything or notice too late that a certain deadline is much closer than you thought.

• **Read through the transcripts from the current day's courses**. Here you can ask yourself initial questions, mark essentials or transfer points to your learning overview.

• **Organize and structure your notes**. Are several half-written sheets collecting in your pad again? Take five minutes a day to file your material and keep it neat and tidy so it's ready when you start your exam preparation.

• **Actively process** the **learning material**. Do exercises. Mark in color. Add notes. Engage in active reading. Ask questions. In the *Learning to Learn* section, some of the techniques you can use will be explored in more detail.

Optimize work phases

In order to build your work blocks efficiently, find one or more fixed **workplaces that are dedicated only to work**. Your bed or sofa are associated with relaxation and leisure activities, consequently avoid such places where something else usually happens. As described above, you can arrange your material in a certain way to create work triggers.

You should also set yourself a certain activity-break rhythm. You can use the **Pomodoro technique for** this. In the previous section, work phases of about half an hour were mentioned more frequently. This is because this is approximately the duration over which people can concentrate well. After that, their energy decreases drastically and they are much easier to distract.

If work phases become too long, you will become increasingly unproductive the longer you sit at a task. The only additional problem is that even if you take a break, you'll start again at a lower energy level than at the very beginning of the block. With the Pomodoro method, you always take a break exactly when your concentration starts to wane, thus keeping your energy level mostly the same. Always work for 25 minutes at a time and then take a 5-minute break. During this recovery period, you should be able to move away from your workstation and relax. Repeat this unit four times so that you have worked for two hours at the end.

After these two hours, you deserve a longer break.

For this, perhaps consider a small reward such as a conversation with your roommate, something tasty to eat, or a short nap.

Learning to learn

Exam preparation is usually associated with staring at hours and hours of transcripts, slides, and notes, reading through them over and over again with the hope of being able to reproduce everything exactly as possible at the end. There are much more effective and personal methods to acquire, connect and remember knowledge.

When learning, you should always **take an active role**. Don't just let words come at you, but ask yourself questions about the content beforehand. What exactly needs to be understood and retained? Basically, this can only be one of two types of information: Facts or concepts.

Facts only have to be learned by heart. Concepts are usually more important to understand. At the same time, you should be able to reproduce them in your own words using the correct terminology. Break down what it is basically about. Classify how different facts and new concepts relate to what you already know. For example, are there connections of ideas? Try to further refine the knowledge and make it more vivid by connecting it to your everyday life and looking for concrete examples in real life that can be explained by what you have learned.

Creatively incorporate **different stimuli.** Use pictures, photos, or mind maps. If you have a penchant for word melodies, make up rhymes or look for words that sound like the terms you want to remember. Think up the shortest, wackiest stories possible from the list of terminology you want to learn. Mnemonic devices or acronyms, where letters abbreviate your fact list or long names, are also great for learning facts. "Seven, five, three - Rome hatches from the egg" is something everyone has heard in history class. Complicated names like European community action scheme for the mobility of university students can be remembered much more easily with the short word ERASMUS.

Additionally, **learning triggers** can be a good way to regularly become aware of content that is difficult to remember. To create such triggers at home, first observe your behavior. In which places do you often spend time? What objects do you often have in your hand? Where do you often look? Then think about what behavior or information should be triggered.

Finally, it's about getting creative and preparing

the triggers. Have tea first thing in the morning at the kitchen table and want to get your appointments in your head more regularly? Put your planner right next to your teacup in the evening. Do you have a list of dates you need to study for a lecture? Tape it to the bathroom mirror at eye level. Keep at it and adjust your triggers when you realize they aren't working the way you want after all.

Test yourself - no matter what point you're at in your exam preparation, the sooner the better. Summarize what you've learned. Try to teach it to someone else. Do exercises. Use index cards. Set aside your transcripts and recall what you read. If you prefer to write, you can also just write down everything you notice in an unstructured way and then match that with your notes.

Retain unpleasant learning material

Time and again, there are topics that you really don't feel like working on - that was the case in school, and it won't be any different in college. Take the following steps to make working with this material more enjoyable:

• Find out why you don't like the subject. Is it because

of the content? Is it because it seems like endless lists of facts to you? Do you not see the relevance to your studies? Or are you generally bothered by the aesthetics of the course's supporting material?

• For these reasons, formulate problem statements with possible solution, which you can approach realistically: "For topic X, I will ask my lecturer where it can influence my studies. For topic Y, I will look into how I can learn facts even more easily" and so on.

• Stay organized and keep your stuff neat and tidy. Maybe make it extra nice so that it looks more inviting to you?

• Begin gently to approach the subject. You don't have to immediately insert a huge block of work within which you go over and over this course. Take small steps. Start by planning your work. Underline and highlight in your transcripts. Jot down initial questions.

• Look for the sides of the subject that appeal to you. Find movies that are remotely related to it. Download apps with educational games about it. Design a quiz with friends using key terms.

• Make positive experiences out of your involvement with the subject. Create a calm and comfortable environment or think of a small reward for afterwards, for example.

• Stay consistent. Do just a little bit, but do it regularly.

• Seek help. If you are absolutely stuck, can't find a way in and can't find anything positive about the subject, turn to friends, fellow students or the teaching staff. There will always be a way to deal with a problem!

TOO MUCH TO READ

You've created working routines, written prioritized to-do lists, and structured your work blocks according to the Pomodoro method, and yet you still can't manage to efficiently fight your way through the mountain of secondary literature? Do you have a reading-intensive course of study so that you can't even think about secondary literature because of all the primary sources?

Or you have a term paper due on a topic you have hardly dealt with before? In this part you will be given some techniques that should help you to work through stacks of books more quickly. Here we distinguish between reading strategies and reading techniques. Reading strategies are procedures that mainly describe how to approach a text. Reading techniques concern the way the actual reading process looks.

Reading Strategies

No matter how and which text you want to approach, you should always prepare the reading process. In addition to specific timing and text selection, you should think carefully about what information you want to get from reading in the first place. What is your goal? Do you just want to compile a bibliography for your upcoming term paper? Do you want to understand the main points of the text? Or are you concerned with having all the details grasped and thought through? Then, depending on your goal, choose the appropriate technique for your needs. Work through the texts and reflect afterwards on the basis of your notes whether your questions have been answered.

Overview reading

The goal of this reading strategy is to get through texts quickly while being able to search for specific information - for example, whether the monograph in your hands is suitable as a source for an essay. So basically, only the structure and rough contents need to be grasped.

In addition, overview reading should also be the

first step if you already know that you want to work through, for example, a certain part of a book in detail. Overview reading helps you to arrange the fragments into an information network. To do this, first look at the most striking features of the text.

What is the material about? Look at the title, the author, the back of the book, and the table of contents. How is the text organized? Then flip through the entire text. How is it organized? What does it look like? Is there an abstract that prefaces the text and briefly introduces it? What are subheadings? Are there graphics or photos?

Are relevant points highlighted or summarized in boxes? Feel free to make brief notes on whether the text is promising or already raises questions. That way, you can also keep track later of which texts you judged to be unsuitable. Look at the next one or stay with the original material and work through it using the appropriate reading technique.

Excerpt reading

Without realizing it, you have already applied the Pareto principle in overview reading. This is also called the 80-20 rule and describes - in terms of text work - that about 80 percent of the content can be found in 20 percent of the text[2] . Thus the excerpt reading is so to speak a continuation of the overview reading. It is particularly suitable for editing articles, but can also be applied to books. In the first step, read the first and last paragraphs of the article completely.

In longer publications, such as monographs, this would correspond to the first and last bullet points of each chapter. Here, the structure, the central topics and the most relevant findings of the text can already be found in a kind of introduction and conclusion.

If it doesn't fit what you're looking for, you can put the article aside at this point. However, if it is suitable, the second step is to read the first sentence of each paragraph in the text. Here you will find more detailed information and keywords. You can also mark particularly interesting paragraphs.

Now you have gained a sufficient picture of the text and know what it deals with for the most part. Maybe this information is already enough for you? Otherwise, you can either read the highlighted paragraphs or the text in its entirety again. The advantage and goal of this strategy, however, is that you do not

---

[2] Cf. Werner Heister: Studying with Success. Efficient Learning and Self-Management in Bachelor, Master and Diploma Programs. Stuttgart: Schäffer-Peoschel Verlag 2007, p. 55.

have to read through the entire text and thus save an enormous amount of time.

Active reading

Active reading can almost be seen as a reading technique, but because of its focus on interaction with the text, it describes more of an approach to the reading process. It is particularly suitable if you want to work through texts meticulously, as it can increase your focus and ability to concentrate. As with various learning techniques, this reading strategy is about using a physical action to engage more senses and thus increase your attention. These are three methods you can use to read more actively:

• Summarize: Read one paragraph at a time. When you finish it, or notice that your thoughts are wandering from the text, summarize that paragraph right in the margin next to it. This can be one word or a whole bullet point. It is important that you equally think directly along in the reading process and break down the text for yourself. These marginal notes can then also serve as an outline for your notes later, but are basically just there for you to interact with the text.

• Instant repetition: Again, the idea here is to be more active by writing things down. This method is especially useful for memorizing facts. Read your bullet points or filter out those of a text. Then take out a scratch paper and try to reproduce this kind of list. Write down everything you remember. It's okay to make this look messy. The main thing is to engage your sense of touch through movement. Now check with the help of the text and add what you have not remembered. You can also do this exercise several times in a row to memorize facts.

• Visible analysis: This method will make it easier for you to go through texts. It can be used for literature, but also your transcripts or the instructor's slides. Read through your material and edit as you go. Paint different topics with corresponding colors. Draw small pictures next to them as everyday examples of the material covered. Think about a drawing system that you can use to mark essential places in the margins of the page. This is where your creativity comes in.

Reading Techniques

This section briefly discusses three reading techniques that you can use to actually read through texts. These techniques are: skimming, skip reading, and speed reading. All three techniques are designed to allow you to avoid wasting time and concentration by reading your material aloud, word by word, in your head.

Fly over

Skimming is basically about letting the text pass before your eye and picking out salient content. For example, you can let your eye glide across the page, targeting different things like the nouns you use. Focus on these. From this, an understanding will start to come together. Another way to skim the text is the slalom technique. This is related to the paragraph reading strategy. Again, you fly over the lines, but read the beginning and end of each paragraph more carefully.

Jumping technique

Since our eyes can hardly move fluently on their own anyway, the skip technique is a good way to read more efficiently[3] . Here, the focus you need per line to pick up should be kept as low as possible.

First, choose your distance from the text so that

---

[3] Cf. Tony Buzan: Speed Reading. Read faster, understand more, retain better. 6th ed. Munich: Wilhelm Goldmann Verlag 2007, p. 66ff.

you can capture multiple words with one focus. It helps to place the first focus point not quite at the beginning of the line and the last one before the actual end of the line. The goal now is to be able to read a line with two to three fixations. For training, you can draw straight lines across the page with a pencil, for example, if you do not want to do this, or a so-called reading aid is recommended as an additional aid. Take a thin, longer object and tap on the page where you want to focus. Among other things, a chopstick could serve as a very simple reading aid.

Speedreading

Speedreading is where you increase your overall reading speed. Always read a little faster than you would on your own. Again, the reading aid is useful here, making it easier for your eyes to coordinate.

It is virtually indispensable. In addition to this, training with the help of a metronome is definitely advisable. You can also find such metronomes free of charge and digitally on the Internet or as an app.

Now glide over the lines in this measure with your reading aid. You can start a new line whenever the metronome beats. Increase the tempo over time. There is even a more special training method where you intentionally set the metronome tempo much higher than you can still understand the text. This creates an effect as if you were driving off a highway. The speed in the city, which seemed fast to you before you left the highway, suddenly seems much slower. Read for a while and then slow down the metronome again. For example, you can reread the passage you just worked on. You will notice that it suddenly becomes much easier for you to read quickly as well.

Ten steps to more success in your studies

What should you definitely take away from this book? Here's a ten-point plan that will guide you to a more balanced daily study routine.

- Think of your studies as your work and make thoughtful decisions.
- Create realistic habits and routines instead of resorting to quick fixes.
- Set up a workspace that is tailored to you and used

primarily for your studies.

• Make timely work and learning plans with specific and actionable goals.

• Sit in the front row to increase your activity.

• Ask yourself questions when you approach a topic.

• Create a learning map to be prepared before you have to be at the latest.

• Make university-related contacts and find like-minded people.

• Work with the Pomodoro technique and reward yourself.

• Use learning and reading strategies and adapt them to your mechanisms.